kELS0's [Black] Book of Poems

kELS0's [Black] Book of Poems
A Poetry Prequel

~ Kelsey Jan Gaither ~

● Nashville, T.N.//2022 ●

Kaffeeklatsch
- BOOKS -

----

kELSO's [Black] Book of Poems: A Poetry Prequel

Copyright © 2022 by Kelsey Jan Gaither

Photo & Art Credit: Kelsey Jan Gaither

English/Young Adult/Poetry
Age Range: 13-18+
Grade Level: 8-12

40 Pages
5,392 Word Count

First Edition

ISBN: 9798809168182
Library of Congress Control Number: 2022907041

www.Amazon.com
Printed by Amazon | KDP (Kindle Direct Publishing) | in the U.S.A.

www.KelseyJan.LiveJournal.com
Kelsey Jan | Kaffeeklatsch | Nashville, T.N.

Disclaimer: Author is the sole writer and poet of the entire text belonging to this literary work of writing in this book of poems and poetry collection. Any information used or portrayed in this collection of poetry is a matter of the author's own personal thoughts, ideas, opinions, and imagination—which have been formulated to, thus, hypothetically try to explain and describe some of life's philosophical and conceptual entailments, such as the commonly known expression of various feelings and ideas, in an elaborate and abstract form of interpretive creative writing. Readers should not take the author's ideas as anything literal, or as a matter of fact, but are instead encouraged to use any reasoning found of their own to, perhaps, gain further introspect and speculation into newly discovered ideas, as they read through and enjoy this modern work in literary poetic art. This highly-stylized form of written literature is produced through the creative writings of select rhythmic and rhymed groupings of wordings, or stanzas, thus, illustrated, performed, and further carried out by the author's own workings, through the written word of poetry, as a literary form of beauty and art.

Author is the sole and entire owner of all the rights to this book.

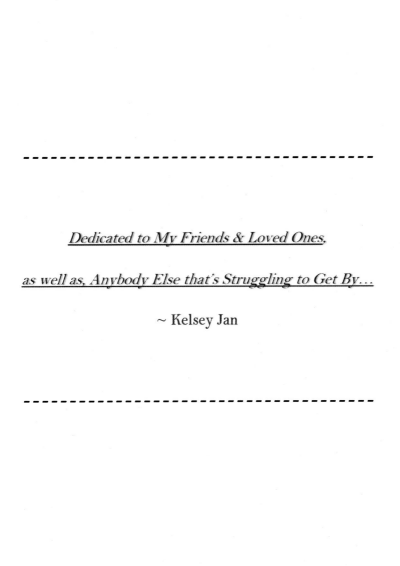

Dedicated to My Friends & Loved Ones,

as well as, Anybody Else that's Struggling to Get By...

~ Kelsey Jan

~ CONTENTS ~

Kelsey Jan Gaither

"I want to make a statement
that stops you in your tracks
and makes you think...
I want to be needed.
I want to help someone make
a difficult decision.
I want to blow someone away...
I want to be deep.
I want to make a difference
in someone's life.
I want to take your breath away"

YEAR of
2006

OPENING STATEMENT

XOXO. kelso.

OPENING STATEMENT ("kELSO's Quote"):

I want to *make* a **statement** that **stops** *you* in your *tracks* & makes you *think*...
I want to be *needed*. I want to help **someone** make a *difficult* decision.
I want to **blow** someone *away*... I want to be *deep*.
I want to make a **difference** in someone's *life*.
I want to **take** your *breath away*. <333

Kelsey Jan Gaither

Hide behind your shades & pretend everything's okay.

Don't try & Fix me. I'm not Broken.

Suddenly i find im not sleeping

Go ahead & be stuck up & let things go to your head. It's not like your going to have friends in the end.

Broken

Broken

Make me your everything

your HATE is always stronger towards the people you once loved.

everything will be alright

Just when i thought love had given up on me

I realized that I had given up on love.

Broken

I don't know if you loved me.
But, I loved you.

I don't know if you truly wanted to be with me.
But, I wanted to be with you.

I don't know if you *even* cared.
But, I did.

Guess the moral of this story is, *at least I tried it.*

------------------------------------ **fREAkiN' l0NG P0EM.**
(kELS0's "poemy thing")

I remember a time.
I remember a place.
I remember the age.
I remember his face.
The late nights.
The loud yelling.
The hate I had.
For the world.
That unfairly ruined the childhood of a little girl.
Lost inside and so confused.
I wasn't sure exactly what to do.
All day and all night the anger would just boil inside.
Between my father's yelling and my mother never there.
I'm not sure exactly which one was more unfair.
A little girl's childhood had to be stopped.
I was forced to grow up too fast in this time clock.
So unsure and not informed.
Of the life that I was much too young to endure.
Limited on friends.
And basically a loner.
I learned the meaning of being truly depressed and unwanted.
Unhappy with life and never satisfied.
My mother tried to help.
But, just made me wanna die.
The police took my dad away.
And all I did was cry.
Young and confused trying to figure out what to do.
I cut my wrist.
I blackened my fist.
Nothing went right.
All I wanted to do was fight.
Young and naive.
I was everyone's pet peeve.
Made fun of everyday.
I could never be the same.
And for some unknown reason.
That turned out to be a very bad thing.
Just because I acted different.
Just because I acted strange.
Everyone in that school treated me with hate.
And in my mind she was to blame.
Life went by...
But, the hate still remained.
Older and older.
But, still basically the same.
That little girl without a father.
And with a mother that never treated her like a daughter.

Unwanted.
Hated.
Finally, I decided to toss the dice.
I changed my life.
But, the way it was done still made no sense.
Just because I dressed different.
I changed my clothes.
I dyed my hair.
I wore make up.
I got friends.
But, still the same person on the inside.
Lost.
Confused.
Hateful.
To their lies...

Were they really my friends?
I'm still not sure to this day.
And that is the problem with this world.
Everyone talks about everyone.
No matter the cost.
Everyone has a past.
Nobody thinks about themselves last.
Everyone has problems.
It is just the way they decide to solve them.
Think about the weird girl the sits behind you in class.
She probably goes home every night and cuts her wrists with glass.
So, the next time you feel like making fun of someone.
Think of this poem.
And then maybe the world will change its hateful and deceitful ways.
And everyone will look back at you in a daze.
Amazed by how nice you were.
How friendly and true.
And hopefully, you can help someone decide what to do.
When you have a friend that is in need.
Do your best to give them what they please.
I have found love.
And I am now wanted.
But...
What I went through.
Was not fair at all.
And NOBODY deserves to be treated like that.
No matter how ugly or fat.
The things people come up with are so sad and immature.
So, people...
Please try to act your age.
Talk to your friends.
Ask them about their past.
Ask them if they are truly okay.
You might be surprised at what they may say........

~ Kelsey Jan Gaither ~

----------------- Mental Institution -----------------

Lost and confused to why I'm here.
I miss my friends so close and dear.
Longing to go home and have a good time.
Yet, so many thoughts rush through my mind.
What did I do to get myself here?
I feel like I've lost the wheel and cannot steer.
I look through the window at the shadows that crawl.
I think about the people and just want to bawl.
The city lights twinkle with fun.
Yet, I have no smile and there is no Sun.
I sit in this room quiet and dead.
Wishing that somehow I could just go to bed.
The city lights call for me, but I can't break free.
I am chained down and watched begging on one knee.
I have to make changes this much is true.
But, what if there is nothing I can do?
I know I am smarter and saner than they think.
Can someone please understand and give me a break?
I want this to be over and done with.
I'm not really sure why I get so pissed.
I want out so bad.
God, I am so sad.
Waiting is probably the hardest part.
I'm just, "stuck up," that's what they put on my chart...
The night is dark and screaming with fun.
Yet, I'm unhappy and feel like I'm being held up by a gun.
I want to break away from these chains.
This place is driving me insane.
I can't stop crying.
Inside I feel like I'm dying.
I'm usually so tough.
But, lately it's been so rough.
The music is dead.
There is no light at the end of the tunnel.
And it's starting to get to my head.
I have tried everything to be happy.
But, no matter what I do I feel sappy.
I try to have fun to get things off my mind.
But, when the fun is over, I'm still lost inside.
I fake a smile every day.
To try to avoid people asking me if I'm okay.
Because, if they asked I'm scared of what I would say.
And later on I don't want to have to pay.
But, here I am for trapping my feelings inside.
Maybe, I should just open my mouth and let it ride.
Maybe I'll change, maybe I won't.
Hopefully, I can get my life to go steady and float.
Every once in a while I might breakdown.
But, that is something I can't turn around.
This is just a stage and I'm sure it will pass.
And soon I'll be living on the other side of the grass.
Improvement is everything, and that's what I'll do.
And then, hopefully, I can get out of this zoo...

------- "Cubby" - - - - - - -

I sit here in this cubby,
Feeling not so very lovely.
I want to go home.
I feel so alone.
I want to have fun. I swear I don't have a gun.
The Sun is almost gone. I'm sitting on a thong...
Hiding from the camera. Please tell me why I'm here?
I swear I don't have any beer.
Why do they not understand me?
Who cares if I'm not very dandy? I want to be free,
And not get stung by a bee... I absolutely hate tea.

"My Lover."

~ ~

My eyes are open.
The night is almost through.
Yet, here I am once again thinking about you.
The fun times we have had.
All the good times and the bad.
And even though I fight and bicker.
My love for you just grows thicker.
Some might say that it's just lust.
But, thinking of you makes my heart want to bust.
Because, I know I'm in love and there is nothing I can do.
I never thought I could find someone who is so true.
I'm holding on to all the good things that you say.
And thinking about them all the time during the day.
In the morning, at school, evening, and night.
All I wanna do is just hold you tight.
I'll sit here and wonder if you feel the same way.
Then get on the phone with you and hear about your day.
There is so much to our future that we can't put in line.
I think it's good how we planned it out, but we should also take our time.
It's hard for me to explain all the things I feel inside.
Without you in my life most likely I'd probably die.
You're the true reason my heart still pounds.
You're the true reason I'm happy, as so I have found.
I got my wish on a four-leaf clover.
I finally found someone who completely won me over.
I love you so much. Can't you see?
I am everything I am, because you love me.

~ ~

~ *Kelsey Jan Gaither* ~

I'm Sorry ~~~~~~

I'm sorry I lied.
I'm sorry I cried.
I'm sorry I said die.
I'm sorry I failed.
I'm sorry my heart is pale.
I'm sorry I didn't thank you.
I'm sorry I made you blue.
I'm sorry I didn't say I love you.
I'm sorry you think I'm so wonderful.
I'm sorry I deceived you.
I'm sorry I'm not who I once was.
I'm sorry I can't rise above.
I'm sorry I brought you down.
I'm sorry I made you frown.
I'm sorry that you don't see.
I'm sorry that we can't be.
I'm sorry that I'm so horrible.
I'm sorry I can't see what you see in me.
I'm sorry I tried to be something I'm not.
I'm sorry the words came out wrong.
I'm sorry I can't explain my thoughts.
I'm sorry I'm lost in scattered dots.
I'm sorry I feel for you.
I'm sorry I made you blue.
I'm sorry my love is like a bad disease.
I'm sorry I screwed you over.
I'm sorry you can't see how horrible I can be.
I'm sorry I have failed.
I'm sorry I made you cry.
I'm sorry I said I wanna die.
I'm sorry I messed with your world.
I'm sorry I was selfish.
I'm sorry you don't see it.
I'm sorry I throw a fit.
I'm sorry I'm a bitch.
I'm sorry if you don't agree.
I'm sorry, but I tried.
I'm sorry you didn't listen.
I'm sorry I was right.
I'm sorry, because I wanna set things right.
I'm sorry I'm being selfish.
I'm sorry I wanna be with you.
I'm sorry, because I don't wanna hurt you.
I'm sorry that I'm doing this for me.
I'm sorry I'm holding on to you.
I'm sorry, because you can't see.
I'm sorry I made you love me.

~~~~~~

~ Kelsey Jan Gaither ~

~~~~~~~~~~~~~ **The Truth.** ~~~~~~~~~~~~~

She says nobody cares.
Yet, all of her friends are always there.

She says she isn't addicted.
Yet, she thinks about it all the time.

She says she is fat.
Yet, she wears a size small.

She says nobody likes her like that.
Yet, guys ask for her number all the time.

She says there is always someone better.
Yet, in his eyes nobody stands a chance next to her.

She says her parents don't love her.
Yet, they do everything they can to make her happy.

She says she is an idiot.
Yet, she is the smartest in her class.

She says she has no father.
Yet, he is all over her walls.

She says she has to pay for everything on her own.
Yet, she doesn't pay for the roof over her head.

She says he doesn't love her.
Yet, he is always there for her and would do anything for her.

She says she is limited on friends.
Yet, her yearbook is filled with names and numbers.

She says she is ugly.
Yet, her mom says she is lucky.

She says she never lies.
Yet, I guess I let the truth pass me by...

~~~~~~~~~~~~~~~~~~~~~~~~~~~~~~~~~~~~~~~

~ Kelsey Jan Gaither ~

– Moulin Rouge! (2001).

~ Kelsey Jan Gaither ~

Jealousy.
It's just not fair.
Jealousy.
It's more than I can bear.
The way he looks at her.
As if he doesn't care.
I'm standing right there.
I guess he doesn't notice me.
He thinks I don't have feelings.
Can't he see?
He is the only one I care for.
Sometimes, I think he needs more.
And if I can't satisfy.
I might as well just die.
I'm the one to blame.
It hurts just to hear his name.
I'm not sure what's going through my head.
I am so confused about everything he said.
If he loves me then how can he like someone else?
Why doesn't he just say it?
"I'm lying to you, Kels."
It's so hard letting go.
I love him more than you could ever know.
He is everything I need.
But, if you love someone set them free.

– The Killers. (2004). "Smile Like You Mean It." *Hot Fuss.*

kELSo's [Black] Book of Poems

~ *Kelsey Jan Gaither* ~

die   X . X

lay me down.
down to die.
die b/c of their lies.
lies are hate.
hate determines fate
fate is my fear.
fear will always be here.
here is my heart.
heart that is cold and dark.
dark from the deception.
deception they bring upon.
upon a fairytale is where i wanna be.
be side someone who will care and see.
see me for who i am.
Am i really that bad?
Bad is what they bring.
Bring the hate to my mind.
Mind is full of thoughts.
thoughts rush through.
through the hate and lies.
lies will cause me to die.

die. XP

----

lay me *down.*
down to *die.*
die b/c of their *lies.*
lies are *hate.*
hate determines *fate.*
fate is my *fear.*
fear will always be *here.*
here is my *heart.*
heart that is a *cold* and *dark.*
dark from the *deception.*
deception they bring *upon.*
upon a fairytale is where I wanna *be.*
beside someone who will *care* and *see.*
see me for who I *am.*
am I really that *bad?*
bad is what they *bring.*
bring the hate to my *mind.*
mind is full of *thoughts.*
thoughts rush *through.*
through the *hate* and *lies.*
lies will cause me to *die.*

-------------------------- **"The Road"** --------------------------

I'm at a fork in the road.
Not sure which way I'll go.
One road I have seen before.
And I'm not interested in getting to know it anymore.
This is the road my parents have been on.
It's also the road that broke their bond.
It's a road of depression and death.
A dark road where you lose your breath.
The other road is bright.
And at the end of the tunnel there is always a light.
It will always have someone there by your side.
And if you're in need nobody will pass you by.
You will be happy and grow old.
And the people close to you will mean more to you than gold.
You will make good decisions and always come out on top.
And your smile will never stop.
Yet, here I am not sure which way to go.
It sounds like an easy choice but it's harder than you think you know.
I want to have fun.
But, if I do it the wrong way I will see no Sun.
I'm going to try my best.
And hopefully, as I go I'll figure out the rest.
So, here I go taking one step ahead.
And maybe, I won't end up dead.
Wish me luck.
And we will see whose future is going to suck.

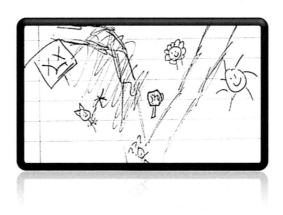

Cutting

4/13/06

The tears fall down.
But I don't make a sound.
The glass separates my skin,
Suddenly my stomach starts to bend.
Relief seeps in.
My pain grows thin.
My mind forgets my troubles.
As the loss of blood doubles.
Nobody gets it.
How could that not even hurt just a little bit?
I have memories of my past.
Life goes by so fast.
And yet for a moment time stops.
My mind plays connect the dots.
I throw on a long sleeve shirt.
If somebody sees it ill feel like dirt.
hide ing a secret under my skin.
Maybe next time i'll use a pin
The scars just bring back the hate.
Maybe this will determine my fate.
Being forced not to do it is just not fair.
Going without it is more than i can bear.

"Cutting"

The tears fall down.
But, I don't make a sound.
The glass separates my skin.
Suddenly my stomach starts to bend.
Relief seeps in.
My pain grows thin.
My mind forgets my troubles,
As the loss of blood doubles.
Nobody gets it.
How could that not even hurt just a little bit?
I have memories of my past.
Life goes by so fast.
And yet for a moment time stops.
My mind plays connect the dots.
I throw on a long sleeve shirt.
If somebody sees it I'll feel like dirt.
Hiding a secret under my skin.
Maybe, next time I'll use a pin.
The scars just bring back the hate.
Maybe, this will determine my fate.
Being forced not to do it is just not fair.
Going without it is more than I can bear.

-------------------- **"Dad"** --------------------

Here I am again,
Not knowing were to begin.
Knowing that he really does care,
It's more than I can bear.
As I grow I mature.
I'm starting to understand the world a little bit more.
I want him in my life.
I want my mom to be his wife.
The more I think about him,
The more I realize I won't win.
I miss him so much.
I can still remember his touch.
Bits and pieces of memories I throw together.
Suddenly, I make him out to be a little bit better.
I have a memory that plays in my head.
One night, I couldn't go to bed.
I stayed up late and waited for him to come home.
I heard the key turn in the front door.
I ran up to greet him.
He picked me up and swung me around.
And for once he didn't have a frown.
I think about that one memory all the time and I don't know why.
I guess, I was just happy that he didn't sigh.
Because, if he sighed that would mean I was annoying him.
And for what he created in my mind, that was a sin.
I know he is better than what they see.
I know deep down he wants the best for me.
I just wish, sometimes, that he was here to see me mature.
To meet my friends.
To be proud of me and love me more.
Sometimes, I feel like there is this hole.
I want to learn more about me and that's the only way to fill my soul.
He is the only person who can completely understand me.
He is my father.
He made me, therefore, I am his daughter.
He is the only person I can have a father, daughter connection with.
But, nowadays, that feels like it's going to be a myth.

I think I love him, but I'm not sure.
That's not enough, though.
I want to know I love him with all my heart.
For he is my father and I wanna know that he will never leave me in the dark.
There are so many people in this world whose fathers are dead.
And I want to take advantage of him still being alive.
And I want him to stand by my side.
Through thick and thin,
It's him who I want to always depend.
But, it's so hard to have that kind of trust.
When your father's lungs are about to bust.
He is killing himself slowly.
And it's starting to take a toll on me, emotionally.
One day he will die.
And I'll never know what it's like to have him by my side.
But, the sad thing is I won't be able to tell the difference.
And the hole inside me will never go away.
And regret and greed will take over and fill that hole.
And then, I won't have a soul to get to know.

- -

- - - - - - - - - - - - - - - Lies - - - - - - - - - - - - - - -

Lies Lies
they are full of shit.
Lies Lies
I want them to die.
Lies Lies
my words are true.
Lies Lies
they said they would listen.
Lies Lies
but, look at it now.
Lies Lies
I did my best.
Lies Lies
and they still act the same.
Lies Lies
nothing has changed.
Lies Lies
I'm still the same.
Lies Lies
I need someone to hold me.
Lies Lies
they say it all the time.
Lies Lies
they were never there for me.
Lies Lies
and I'm not to blame.
Lies Lies
for once I will not put this on myself.
Lies Lies
they said they would help.
Lies Lies
but, look at them.
Lies Lies
they just make it worse.
Lies Lies
I hope they die.

Lies Lies
I truly don't care anymore.
Lies Lies
they said they cared.
Lies Lies
they said they would be there.
Lies Lies
yet, here I am and they're not here.
Lies Lies
and back come all of my fears.
Lies Lies
my problems are back from their nap.
Lies Lies
and nobody is here for me.
Lies Lies
alone by myself.
Lies Lies
I'm slipping back into my old self.
Lies Lies
all b/c of their lies.
Lies Lies
they said they would be here.
Lies Lies
but, they are nowhere to be found.
Lies Lies
they said they would help.
Lies Lies
they said they would listen.
Lies Lies
they said they would compromise.
Lies Lies
I hope they die.
Lies Lies
b/c of their lies.
Lies Lies
bitches.

- -

"Best Friend." <3

~~~~~~~~~~~~~~~~~~~~~~~~~~~~~~~~~

~~~~~~

There is this girl & she is just like me.
We think exactly alike & it can get scary you see.
We understand each other.
She is closer to me than my brother.
I tell her everything that goes through my head.
We have long discussions as we lay in bed.
We are both cancers, so we see eye-to-eye.
We have conversations of what it will be like when we die.
She is like a sister to me.
And that's the way I would like it to be.
She has an amazing personality.
We both, sometimes, get lost in reality.
I would do anything for her this is true.
If she needed help I would do what I could do.
If anyone messed with her I would beat them black & blue.
I never saw us being this great of friends.
And I hope this friendship won't meet its end.
She is my best friend & I don't know what I would do without her.
The best times we have spent together are still a blur.
She is my party buddy.
I go to her house & we never study.
We came from totally different backgrounds.
Yet, we are exactly the same all around.
I don't want her to fade into another face in the crowd.
When we are together we always get so loud.
I love her with all of my heart.
And I hope that we never part.

~~~~~~

~~~~~~~~~~~~~~~~~~~~~~~~~~~~~~~~~~~~

- - - - - - - - - - - - - - - - **"My Words"** - - - - - - - - - - - - - - - -

Trapped inside with nowhere to go.
Being young is harder than you think you know.
Listen to me when I talk.
You'll be surprised when you see the secrets my words unlock.
My words are strong, my intentions are dear.
I can take away any of your fears.
Give me a chance and maybe you'll learn who I am.
But, you must remain as silent as a lamb.
Listen and you will understand.
On the inside I'm flawed and I need a hand.
My life is going nowhere.
My heart feels bare.
People say they really do care.
Yet, I know they have their own problems so why bother them with mine?
Then again... What problems? My life is just fine.
I create my own problems and it's driving me insane.
My heart is broken and I can't stop the rain.
My heart is broken and it feels so much pain.
And I don't mean broken as in I have lost someone I love.
I mean broken as if I'm being punished from above.
My soul is as free as a dove.
Yet, so much sorrow follows me and fits me like a glove.
I wish I could smile and mean it.
But, every time I try it just doesn't fit.
Yes, I am young, but do I care?
I have never cared about myself and it's easy to bear.
I haven't sat down and thought about where I wanna be in 5 years.
And as blunt as it might sound, some people think about it in fear.
But, for me I just hope it's anywhere, but here.
I want people to take me serious.
Instead of looking at me so delirious.
Trust me when I tell you things.
My eyes do not lie behind my bangs.
Somebody once told me that God gave us 2 ears and 1 mouth for a reason.
And I will listen throughout every season.
But, every now and then I need a moment to tell my side.
I need someone to listen, because I know you can't read my mind.
So, all I ask is for you to listen.
Then, maybe I'll have a true smile and it will glisten.

- -

Lost Without You...

It's my fault, b/c I let go.
And now I'm paying for it, b/c I miss you, so.
I'd rather die than see you with her.
She took you away from me, as if she took away my fur.
I told her it was okay.
And now I'm paying for it every day.
I have been lying to myself.
I said it was okay for you to go with someone else.
I tried to give you the best.
But, I didn't think through the rest.
I hope you're as happy as you make it out to be.
B/c I'm miserable, as so it seems.
My heart will be the death of me.
All b/c it can't set you free.
Every boy has taken me & shoved.
All I ever wanted was just to be loved.
And with you I thought I found my everything.
"You are killing me softly," my heart had sang.
But, then you played around.
My heart was crushed & death is where I was bound.
I'm so confused, & don't know what to do.
I want you back, so please give me a clue.
I am living a lie.
All I ever do is cry.
I miss you so much.
I especially miss your touch.
You are my best friend.
And I don't want us to meet our end.
I guess I'm just scared.
I really don't think you ever cared.
I am so lost inside.
All I wanna do is stay in my room & hide.
So, I guess my point is I'm still in love with you.
And I want you back, so tell me what I should do?

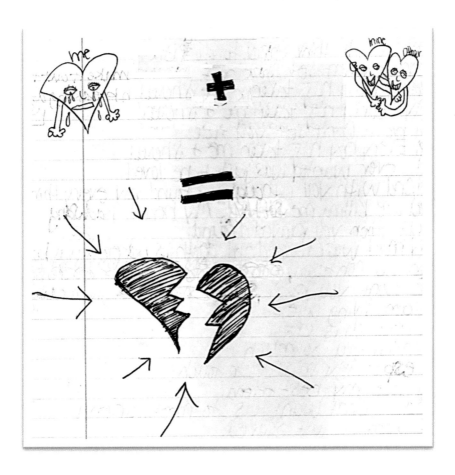

A Good Friend =) -

He is using drugs to hide.
Yet, I will always stand by his side.
He wants to go back to where he used to be.
I want him here, but he can't see.
There are so many people that love & care for him here.
I just wish he could be happy & stand out with no fear.
I look in his eyes & it makes me wanna cry.
Inside his eyes all it looks like is he wants to die.
I wish he could be happy & smile all the time.
But, instead, he just looks depressed & full of crime.
He could be so amazing if he could just let loose.
But, when it all comes down to it, it's him who has to choose.
I know he finds it mean & unfair.
But, if he would just loosen up then we could be the same as up there.
He has so much potential if he could just take it & run.
I love & care about him & I wanna prove that he can have fun.
I understand that he misses his friends.
But, if he would look right in front of him he would see people lending him hands.
Hopefully, he will learn & see us all here.
And then his eyes will be filled with happiness & he will find his true friends close & dear.

- -

\\\

you think that you know me,
but you have no idea…
you say you care,
but you know you really don't…
so, go ahead & lie to me,
you know you are good at it anyway…
you think I'm naïve,
but I can see straight through your lies…
so, I'll just lie to myself, also.
I'll put a smile on my face,
and we can just pretend everything's okay…

///

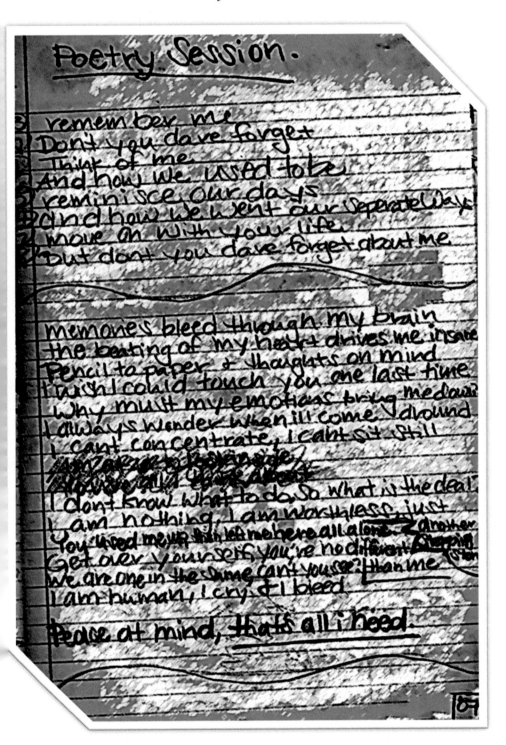

Poetry Session.

remember me
Don't you dare forget
Think of me
And how we used to be
reminisce our days
and how we went our separate ways
move on with your life
but don't you dare forget about me.

memories bleed through my brain
the beating of my heart drives me insane
Pencil to paper + thoughts on mind
I wish I could touch you one last time
Why must my emotions bring me down?
I always wonder when ill come around
I cant concentrate, I cant sit still

I dont know what to do so what is the deal?
I am nothing, I am worthless, just
You used me up then left me here all alone another
Get over yourself you're no different
We are one in the same cant you see? than me
I am human, I cry + I bleed

Peace at mind, that's all i need.

Process of the mind — — —
She is cautious with a broken heart
taking life day by day _____ inside
facing her fears in hurtful ways
She is broke down & bruised
trying to heal her own wounds
making the best of what she's go
pacing away at life's time clock
Live life & be happy they tell her
She is so sick of those cold decein
Trying to forget the memories that —
haunt ~~her~~
Attempting a smile, but she cannot
Cover it up with fakeness so golder
She knows its ~~~~ not gonna hurt
when she's frozen
hollow inside just trying to make it by
~~~~ Taking it day by day, enjoy
the tide...

(trying to)

Poetry Session.

---

❸ remember me
❷ don't you dare forget
❶ think of me
❻ and how we used to be
❺ reminisce our days
❹ and how we went our separate ways
❼ move on with your life
❽ but don't you dare forget about me

~~~~~~

Memories bleed through by brain
The beating of my heart drives me insane
Pencil to paper and thoughts on mind
I wish I could touch you one last time
Why must my emotions bring me down?
I always wonder when I'll come around
I can't concentrate, I can't sit still
I don't know what to do, so what is the deal?
I am nothing, I am worthless, just another steppingstone
You used me up, then left me here all alone
Get over yourself, you're no different than me
We are one in the same, can't you see?
I am human, I cry and I bleed

Peace at mind, that's all I need.

~~~~~~

Process of the mind - - -
She is cautious with a broken heart inside
Taking life day by day
Facing her fears in hurtful ways
She is broke down and bruised
Trying to heal her own wounds
Making the best of what she's got
Pacing away at life's time clock
Live life and be happy they tell her
She is so sick of those cold Decembers
Trying to forget the memories that haunt
Attempting a smile, but she cannot
Cover it up with a fakeness so golden
She knows it's not gonna hurt when she's frozen
Hollow inside, just trying to make it by
Taking it day by day, trying to enjoy the ride...

"<u>Break-ups</u>."

~~~~~~
~~~~~~~~~~~~~~~~~~~~~~~~~

Life goes on,
Even with you gone.
Never thought I would make it to tomorrow.
But, for some reason I'm getting over this sorrow.
I'm gonna make it to see better days.
I am sick of always having to change my ways.
With you gone I now have time for myself, so I've found.
I'm no longer under your lockdown.
I know I wasn't perfect.
But baby, wasn't it worth it?
We went through a lot and changed for the best.
We held our heads high and said, "Fuck the Rest."
We grew in our own time.
And found out we would be just fine.
You are still my dear friend.
And you will remain in my heart, as I mend. <3

~~~~~~~~~~~~~~~~~~~~~~~~~
~~~~~~

"Never change, *unless* you
are **hurting** yourself..." <3

~ (Kelsey, 2005) ~

Author/Poet's name is Kelsey Jan Gaither—*(also known by her pen name, Kelsey Jan)*—and was born on July 12, 1991. She was raised in Tennessee and currently still lives there today with her cat, Zahari... "I came from a low-income, single parent home. In my teenage years, I started writing poetry as a coping mechanism to help me better deal with my severe clinical depression, as suggested by doctor. In my youth, I was the quiet and reserved type, and poetry helped me get outside of myself a little more, by writing my innermost thoughts and feelings down onto paper—allowing me a positive source of outlet and means of self-expression.

I began using my poetry writings as a way of journal keeping, writing about major life events by using vague and symbolic metaphors and rhymes to express my deepest, innermost thoughts and feelings on pressing matters—something like writing in code. Later in life, once I had battled and eventually overcame my severe issues with depression, my poetry then shifted from the dark, distraught, and more heavy-felt, deeper topics towards more of the lighter sense of topics—*involving personal over-comings, peace, and overall, love.* As my relationships and bonds grew deeper and stronger, they also took that of a more serious tone, as comes with time and age.

My writing is always left somewhat abstract, as to allow personal interpretation for each of its readers. I love the art of how one person can read one thing and apply it to their own personal life and get something out of it, and someone else can read the same exact thing and get something completely different out of it, than that which the other person did. Every poem I write is like a little piece of myself, parts of my soul, and often depicts a serious topic, event, or challenge within my own personal life.

In college, I began as a major in 'Philosophy,' wanting to study the great minds of famous thinkers of our past and expand, or explore, upon specific personal interests and ideas within my own life. I later, however, changed majors—my good eye, great sense of taste, and love for aesthetics won out and I chose 'Interior Design,' as my main career field. My great interest and deep-seeded love for creative-writing never has ceased, though. I still continue on with my personal writings in my spare time, jotting down little interests and ideas, making rhythms and rhymes as I go...

I hope my writing has the ability to incite and cure the thoughts and minds of its readers. Containing highly-relatable experiences and issues within its descriptions, so eloquent and simplistically written as to leave no confusion to its readers, making it possible for any person to relate and understand the topics explored in this poetry collection piece."

Thank You for Reading!

~Kelsey Jan ☺

KelseyJan.Designs@Gmail.com
KelseyJan.LiveJournal.com

◊ More Books by the Author ◊
~ Kelsey Jan Gaither ~

~~~~~~~~~~~~~~~~~~~~~~~~~~~~~~~~~~~~~~~

– Poetry Book Collections –

Kelsey Jan Poetry Series:
(Book 1 & 2)

"Love," Written On the Cover... {(Book of Poetry)}
kELSO's [Black] Book of Poems: A Poetry Prequel

– Children's Novels –

A Fairy's Tale

– Additional Publications –

Poem, "TIME," seen in book, *Walk of Life: Anthology of Poems,*
by Poets' Choice, in year 2021, p. 67-68.

~~~~~~~~~~~~~~~~~~~~~~~~~~~~~~~~~~~~~~

Made in the USA
Columbia, SC
17 February 2023

12164361R00029